WHITE SANDS

NATIONAL MONUMENT

Rose Houk and Michael Collier

WESTERN NATIONAL PARKS ASSOCIATION

TUCSON • ARIZONA

ACKNOWLEDGMENTS

The authors wish to thank the staff at White Sands National Monument for their assistance on this project. John Mangimeli and Bill Fuchs led us to information, helped with logistics, and responded to many requests. Steve Fryberger provided a thorough review of the geologic portion of the text. Personnel at the White Sands Missile Range also graciously cooperated by supplying information and photographic opportunities. T. J. Priehs, Ron Foreman, and Sandra Scott of Southwest Parks and Monuments Association got the project going and saw it through the publication process. Our sincere thanks to one and all.

Copyright © 1994 by Western National Parks Association

Published by Western National Parks Association

The net proceeds from WNPA publications support educational and research programs in the national parks.

Receive a free Western National Parks Association catalog, featuring hundreds of publications. Email: info@wnpa.org or visit www.wnpa.org

ISBN 1-877856-50-9

Library of Congress Number 94-67912

Editorial: Sandra Scott

Photography: Michael Collier

Design: Larry Lindahl

Maps and diagrams: Deborah Reade—pages 10, 12, 13, 18, 20, 21, 26, 51, 63.

Illustration: Larry Lindahl—pages 43, 44, 45, 50.

Additional photography:
Center for Southwest Research, General Library, University of New Mexico, 000-021-0052—page 50.
Robert and Linda Mitchell—Chihuahuan desertscrub, page 26; pronuba moth, 28; creosote bush, 36–37.
Museum of New Mexico—page 52.
New Mexico State University Library, Rio Grande Historical Collections—Fall and Rhodes, page 54.
National Park Service—Sandstorm, page 15; McKee, 18; 40, 41 42, 49; Lee, 53; Charles, panorama, 54; 55.
Laurence Parent—page 48.
University of Texas at El Paso, Special Collections—Garrett, Jose and Felipe Lucero, page 53.
White Sands Missile Range—pages 58, 59, 60, 61.

Printed by Imago

Printed in Singapore

Cover photo:
Soaptree yucca in the white sands. San Andres Mountains on horizon.

Contents

Traces in the Sand

From the surrounding mountains, a shimmering white expanse is visible in the desert below. It is not a mirage, but gleaming dunes of white sand. This dune field is one of the largest in the United States, covering nearly three hundred square miles. The sand of the dunes is not the usual quartz, but nearly pure gypsum, fine as sugar when it sifts through your fingers. Take a walk across the dunes in springtime and you will find their surface firm, not soft as are most sands.

White Sands is a place that plays tricks on your imagination. Distances deceive. The barrenness is surreal. Everything seems artful and

Left to right:
**Bird tracks in sand.
Soaptree yucca.
Lesser earless lizard.
Arcs inscribed in sand
by windblown grass.**

deliberately composed: black seeds on white sand; the mosaic of tiny rocks covering an anthill; the crescent moon above violet dunes; a single bright pink wildflower, timing its life to the rhythm of the rains.

Life is not at all obvious here. It is implied, or twice removed, and must be read in signs or code. Ripple marks tell of the wind's way with individual sand grains. Footprints, mounds, and burrows bespeak the presence of mice, pocket gophers, and foxes. A single bird flashes from the top of one yucca stalk to another. Graceful arcs are etched into the sand by swaying grass stems. After a rain, reflections sparkle in salty pools of water that fill the flat places between the dunes. Plants growing atop solitary pedestals of hardened gypsum testify to the struggle to avoid a sandy burial.

It is wonderful to wander and play in the white sands, shedding your cares with your shoes, and trying to guess at some of nature's clues. As you continue, just one dune over, voices and laughter are absorbed into the complete stillness. The blue mountains on the horizons, like silhouetted cutouts, help you keep your bearings.

But beware of wandering too far. There is, for all practical purposes, no suitable water to drink.

Temperatures can soar to 100 degrees Fahrenheit in summer, and there is precious little shade. As you venture deeper into the dune field, one dune soon begins to look exactly like another. Should clouds move in, the mountains can disappear, and with them all points of reference.

As you walk, you may begin to wonder why these dunes are here and how life manages to survive among them. The existence of this extensive, unusual dune field is due to a specific combination of factors: an enclosed basin in a warm climate, a source of gypsum, and wind. The Tularosa Basin is flanked on the east and west sides by mountain ranges from which water flows intermittently, carrying great quantities of dissolved gypsum. This gypsum concentrates in Lake Lucero, an ephemeral lake, frequently dry by late spring each year. After gypsum crystals are formed within the lakebed, they are set in motion by ferocious winds that pile up grains in elegant dunes as high as sixty feet. The few plants that can grow here are those able to survive constant movement of their homes. Animals have adapted too, using fascinating strategies.

Work of the Wind

Mare's tail clouds have drifted from one horizon to the other all morning: feathery white brush strokes high against a deep blue sky. The clouds promise a change in weather. The wind is beginning to kick up. From a vantage point atop a fifty-foot sand dune, you can hear puffs of wind rattling the leaves of the cottonwood that grows at the base. Stronger gusts are blowing out of the southwest—ten, fifteen, even twenty miles an hour.

Sand grains bounce along the dune's surface; as the wind gains strength, sand sails by, first around your ankles, now almost to your knees. Fine sand and dust rise even higher and obscure the view of the nearby mountains. Blowing sand writhes up the windward side of the dune in streamers that vanish when they reach the top. The sand piles up on the dune's downwind side; the steep lee face can support only so much unconsolidated weight and eventually the highest mound breaks loose, avalanching down

Preceding page: Slipface deposits among dunes.

Avalanche on slipface of gypsum dune.

to the base. The wind peaks at forty miles an hour. Sand is everywhere, infiltrating your clothes and camera, stinging your eyes. Take cover; tuck down a little further into your coat. This is geology in action.

Nearly 20 percent of the earth's land surface can be classified as desert, receiving less than ten inches of precipitation a year. These regions, including White Sands National Monument, generally lie about twenty-five or thirty degrees north or south of the equator. At these latitudes, a persistent subtropical high pressure strongly influences the atmosphere, typically producing clear dry skies.

Other deserts exist in regions that are inland and far removed from marine sources of moisture. Some, like the Great Basin just east of California's Sierra Nevada, lie within the rain shadow cast by large mountain chains. You might think of deserts as endless stretches of barren sand, as in Saudi Arabia or Africa's Sahara. But in reality, only a small fraction of the earth's deserts are covered by dunes. In some places, notably the midriff of Africa just south of the Sahara, dunes are encroaching on land that had previously been habitable. This process of desertification can be

the result of slow changes in climate, but also can stem from overgrazing and other improper land use.

In the United States, two of the largest active dune fields exist in California, one in the Mojave Desert and the other near the mouth of the Colorado River. An even greater dune field lies within the Sand Hills of western Nebraska, but that area now receives twenty inches of rain each year, and vegetation has covered and temporarily stabilized the dunes.

The dunes of White Sands National Monument are unique because they comprise the world's largest expanse of *gypsum* sand dunes. Most of the world's sand is made of quartz, a hard silicon mineral; gypsum, as we will see, is made of calcium and sulfur atoms.

The horizon at White Sands is dominated by two mountain ranges, the Sacramento to the east, and the San Andres to the west. The Sacramento Range is a block of the earth's crust that tilts gently eastward. The western edge of this range is the abrupt line of cliffs seen running north-south from our vantage point at White Sands. This edge is made up of a series of large fractures known as the Alamogordo Fault Zone.

The town of Alamogordo, fifteen miles northeast of White Sands, rides on rocks that have been downdropped at least seven thousand feet from their original position alongside similar rocks in the Sacramento Mountains. This faulting has taken place within the last ten million years or so, relatively recently in a geologic sense. All the same, Alamogordo seems to be a pretty peaceful place to live these days: no earthquakes

BASIN

AND

RANGE White Sands National Monument

White sands with San Andres Mountains.

White Sands lies just within the eastern edge of the Basin and Range geologic province.

greater than a Richter magnitude of 3 have been observed since record-keeping began in 1849.

To the west of White Sands rise the San Andres Mountains. These tilt to the west, in an orientation opposite that of the Sacramentos. The steep eastern face of the San Andres Mountains faces White Sands National Monument; it is also a fault zone, with downdrop occurring on the east side. The two ranges are made up of similar sedimentary rock formations; the mountains were once connected by the same rocks that are now downdropped to form the basin floor.

In both ranges, the rocks are primarily Paleozoic in age, ranging from the oldest Bliss Sandstone (~500 million years old) up to the San Andres Formation (~240 million years old). A few more hundred feet of younger rocks are found atop the San Andres Mountains. Corresponding layers have been stripped off the top of the Sacramentos. The sedimentary formations within the San Andres Mountains perch on top of a conspicuous light-gray layer of older gneiss and granite, and appear as horizontal bands of alternately dark or light rock, some forming prominent cliffs, others forming slopes. The gneiss and granite upon which they rest are Precambrian metamorphic and igneous rocks that do not show the horizontal configuration of the overlying sedimentary layers.

Between the San Andres and Sacramento mountains lies the Tularosa Basin. It stretches 150 miles north to south, and as wide as 60 miles east to west, covering some 6,500 square miles. The San Andres Mountains and the Tularosa Basin mark the easternmost edge of the Basin and Range Province. This important geologic province extends from Oregon, down through Nevada, Utah, Arizona, and northern Mexico, and here into New Mexico. The Basin and Range is an area where the earth's crust has been pulled apart, becoming thinner in the process. Basin-and-range extension in central New Mexico began about 29 million years ago. At the same time that extension was occurring, basement blocks of Precambrian rock began to rotate along steep faults, raising the ranges of Paleozoic rock above the surrounding basins. Sierra Blanca, a twelve-thousand-foot peak at the north end of the Sacramentos, stands more than eight thousand feet above the lowest surface of the Tularosa Basin.

As the Tularosa Basin formed between the intervening mountain ranges, tremendous quantities of sediment were washed down from the mountains. Along the western margin of the basin, drilling has penetrated six thousand feet of loosely consolidated debris that had been flushed down primarily from the San Andres Mountains. At its deepest, the drill hit limestone, sandstone, and shale tentatively identified as the Santa Fe Formation, formed within the last 25 million years. On the east side of the Tularosa Basin, drillers encountered the Santa Fe Formation at a depth of four thousand feet. The drill rig penetrated a short depth beyond the Santa Fe Formation, which was not done on the west side. Drill cuttings from the well suggest that Paleozoic rocks underlie the much younger Santa Fe Formation on the east side of the basin. Early geologists, squinting at the faulted margins of the San Andres and Sacramento mountains, assumed that the Tularosa Basin had simply and symmetrically collapsed downward, like the center of a fallen cake. They called the basin a *graben*, a down-dropped block bounded by faults. But as happens so often when we look more closely, the basin's history is more complex than originally assumed.

After studying minute local variations in the earth's gravity field as measured at the surface of the Tularosa Basin, geologists have begun to suspect that a buried fault zone separates the eastern and western halves of the basin—suspected but not seen. The floor of the Tularosa Basin is not a simple, single buried layer; it appears to be fractured down the middle, and faulting along the flanks of the Sacramentos and San Andres may have happened not simultaneously, but at different times. You will still hear the Tularosa referred to as a graben, but geologists now qualify the term, using phrases like "two half-grabens" to better describe what they think really exists beneath the basin floor.

Another important aspect of the Tularosa Basin can be observed without sophisticated geophysical instrumentation. Topographic maps of the basin reveal that no streams drain from the basin. Geologists speculate that an early Rio Grande may have once flowed through the southern part of the Tularosa Basin on its way to the Gulf of Mexico. But uplift of the basin margins subsequently excluded the river. The Rio Grande has been securely embedded in its current valley west of the Tularosa for millions of years. And the Tularosa Basin is now without drainage to the sea. Any water that flows into the basin is trapped until evaporation can waft it away. At White Sands, the air is so hot and dry that eighty inches will evaporate from a body of standing water each year.

During late Pleistocene time, this region received much more precipitation than today, and a much larger lake existed here. Dubbed Lake Otero, this body of water was deep enough that its waves cut terraces on ground that is now high and dry above White Sands. The surface elevation of Lake Otero fluctuated but apparently

The fracture and dropping down of underlying rock formed the basin between the San Andres and Sacramento mountains.

VALLEY OF FIRES

A very different kind of liquid flowed into the Tularosa Basin in the not-so-distant past. Little Black Peak lies a few miles northwest of the town of Carrizozo, at the north end of the basin. Beneath this peak is a crack that has at times been forced open by the upwelling of magma—molten rock—from within the uppermost layers of the earth's crust. The lava has roared out onto the surrounding countryside, burning everything in its path, flowing south forty-five miles into the basin. The rock that it formed records the last contorted textures assumed by the lava as it cooled to the point of solidifying into basalt.

Walking across the ropey black surfaces and broken slabs, called malpais (Spanish for "bad land"), you can easily imagine the wild and steaming conflagration that surrounded the lava's arrival into the basin. Geologists have variously estimated the basalt's age between fifteen hundred years (based on the amount of weathering and erosion that appears to have taken place) and five thousand years (based on the orientations of magnetism locked into place within the basalt after the lava flowed into the basin and hardened). Visitors can explore this volcanic landscape at Valley of Fires National Recreation Area near Carrizozo.

Black lava at Valley of Fires.

The map labels include:

N

Chupadera Mesa

▲ Little Black Peak
5,679 feet
■ Valley of Fires
● Carrizozo

El Malpais

Sierra Blanca Peak
12,003 feet ▲

Three Rivers

Quartz Dunes

SAN ANDRES MTS.

TULAROSA BASIN

● Tularosa

SACRAMENTO MTS.

Gypsum Dunes

Alkali Flat

Lost River

WHITE SANDS

● Alamogordo

Lake Lucero

LAKE OTERO

Rio Grande

Las Cruces ●

ORGAN MOUNTAINS

| 0 | 10 | 20 | 30 | 40 | 50 |
MILES

The Tularosa Basin, indicating the ancient Lake Otero and the extent of the current dunefield.

the lake never did overflow the basin; instead, it finally dried up sometime after the end of the Pleistocene. The lowest points of the Tularosa Basin are now covered by Lake Lucero, at the southwest tip of the white sands dune field. The lake is rarely more than a few inches deep, and often dries up and then isn't a lake at all.

Geologists have been exploring the Tularosa Basin and climbing around on its white sands at least since 1891, when R.T. Hill described the dunes and associated groundwater conditions and R.S. Tarr wrote about the dunes and lava

flows in the region. Scientific interest in the area blossomed in 1900 as paper after paper explored the mineral potential of both the basin and surrounding mountains. O.E. Meinzer and R.F. Hare published their classic geologic description of the basin in 1915. They alluded to storm winds plucking gypsum crystals from Alkali Flat and flinging them east onto the dunes. No scientific paper has since been without mention of the wind when discussing the origin of the dunes.

The Tularosa Basin, lacking vegetation of any significant height, offers minimal resistance to

Storm at White Sands.

passing storm. When a stream does manage to reach the basin floor, it quickly soaks in and adds to the groundwater pool that lies beneath the Tularosa Basin surface. Some groundwater emerges from small springs found at the foot of many side canyons. Surprisingly, the water table is quite high throughout this desert basin, usually no more than a few feet below the surface of the dunes. During wet years, the water table may actually be above ground level, and pockets of standing water form small lakes between some of the dunes.

At White Sands National Monument, water quality, not quantity, is the more pressing issue. You might have to dig only a foot or two to reach water, but you would surely think twice about drinking it. As streams flow down from the mountains, they commonly carry dissolved solids in concentrations of 1,000 to 1,500 parts per million (ppm), three or four times the threshold at which one would begin to taste it in water. Shallow wells close to the mountains can produce water with 2,000 to 4,000 ppm dissolved solids. But wells drilled deep into the middle of the Tularosa Basin have produced dissolved solid concentrations in excess of 110,000 ppm.

What are these dissolved solids? South of Alamogordo, there exist the calcium bicarbonates and calcium magnesium bicarbonates that are associated with limestone and dolomite bedrock. Elsewhere in the basin are sodium chloride brines that can dry to form common table salt. But most notably, there are calcium sulfates. The house recipe at White Sands calls for one ion each of calcium and sulfate, mixed with two molecules of water. Voila! $CaSO_4 \cdot 2(H_2O)$, also known as gypsum. Some of the Paleozoic rock layers in the mountains looming above the Tularosa Basin are rich in gypsum—the Panther Seep and San Andres formations have contributed some of this material. But the bulk appears to have been dissolved from thick beds of gypsum within the Yeso Formation of Middle Permian age, some 250 million years old. In the San Andres Mountains northwest of the dunefield, the Yeso Formation is

the wind. Wind here is more than just the movement of air, more than something measured merely in miles per hour. The dunes are the wind made visible.

More often than not, the wind is light, blowing out of the south, east, or west. But when a storm and its associated low atmospheric pressure moves into southern New Mexico, particularly in the springtime, the Tularosa Basin is raked by extremely strong winds out of the southwest. Winds of fifty-five miles an hour are not uncommon in March and April. Alternatively, winds can blow out of the north, but these rarely have the velocity of their southwesterly counterparts.

Storms that do hit the Tularosa are clustered into two periods. Brief but intense thunderstorms from July through September bring the majority of the basin's annual precipitation, while broad frontal storm systems from October through May deliver the remainder of an average year's rainfall. A noticeable gradient of rainfall exists from the monument's eastern to western boundaries: six-and-a-half inches falling on the west side, and up to ten inches falling on the east. High country within the mountains surrounding the basin receives much greater amounts of precipitation.

A few perennial streams drain into the basin, like the Rio Tularosa that flows down from the Sacramento Mountains. But for the most part, the mountains are drained by ephemeral streams, flowing into the basin only in response to a

1,580 feet thick, of which 635 feet are heavily laden with gypsum. Not surprisingly, the word *yeso* is Spanish for "gypsum."

Each year, storms dissolve a bit more gypsum out of the Yeso Formation and wash a few more calcium and sulfate ions down into the basin. Groundwater remains trapped within this enclosed basin, and the concentration of calcium sulfate increases as more minerals are delivered and more free water is extracted by evaporation.

As ancient Lake Otero evaporated, its shores shrank to the approximate dimensions of today's Lake Lucero and then the lake dried up entirely; along the way, the water became a progressively more concentrated brine. When a calcium sulfate brine is evaporated under the right conditions, gypsum can precipitate out as selenite, long, beautiful crystals of gypsum, a mineral that is soft enough to scratch with your fingernail. And selenite crystals

Selenite crystals near Lake Lucero.

Sandstorm.

certainly did grow in the supersaturated mud beneath the remains of Lake Otero.

A remarkable quantity of translucent golden-yellow selenite is found around the margins of Lake Lucero. The crystals can grow to lengths of four feet. They litter the surface, lying in a layer from thirty feet above the water of the present lake to at least a few feet below. When exposed on the surface, the crystals are subject to weathering and erosion. Cycles of freezing and thawing

steadily pop them apart. The wind strips away any fine gypsum powder that spalls from the crystals. This powder can be whipped into clouds a thousand feet high, riding up-valley as a wild, white dust storm. The larger grains are plucked by the wind and bounced along the ground. Each time a grain strikes the ground, its soft surface can be easily nicked. The grain surface, which started out yellow and translucent, becomes opaque white as each nick scatters light that once had been able to pass directly through the crystal.

The grains are driven by the wind toward the dunes of White Sands National Monument. These dunes stretch thirty miles north from Lake Lucero, and are as much as ten miles across. Less than half of the dunes are actually within the national monument, with the remainder being in the White Sands Missile Range. North of the gypsum dunes are other vegetated dunes predominantly made of quartz. This quartz-rich area lies well north of the monument boundaries however.

Hundreds of square miles of white gypsum! In 1925 John Melhase took a long hard look at all this gypsum and concluded that the dunes represented a bonanza to the person who could carry them off to market and sell the gypsum as plaster of paris. Melhase figured that if the dune thickness averaged thirty feet, every square mile ought to hold 33 million tons of 94- to 99.7-percent-pure gypsum. Melhase was standing in the middle of a 278-square-mile dune field. That's a lot of plaster of paris. All he needed was a railroad and a few shovels.

Although some houses in Alamogordo actually were constructed of "White Sands Block," neither Melhase nor any of the many others who had speculated on the value of the dunes ever got around to actually hauling away any significant quantities of gypsum. Herbert Hoover finally laid all speculation to rest when he declared White Sands a national monument in 1933.

The Wind Made Visible

D usk is a magical time amidst the dunes. The sky is transformed by colors missing during the mid-day glare. The sands unveil the soft curves and delicate surface textures that are obscured by the hot white light of noon. Away from any roads, lying on your back and seeing only white dunes and a blue horizon, you are in a world reduced to the essentials of sand and sky. This is not the time to take sand for granted. There is so much of it around. For now, all that matters is sand.

Broadly speaking, sand is defined as a particle that is small and light enough to be easily moved by wind or water, and too large and heavy to stay suspended in the air or current. Anything lighter would be called dust or silt; anything heavier, pebble or gravel. Depending on which authority you consult, sand grains might be as small as 0.1 to 0.2 millimeters, and as large as 1.6 to 2.0 millimeters in diameter.

We tend to think of sand as sediment along a river or along an ocean beach. Most of the sand in the world is composed of the very hard mineral quartz. But by the definition given above, sand can be made of any material—tiny bits of basalt on the black beaches of Hawaii, finely ground sea shells in the Bahamas, or the gypsum grains at White Sands National Monument.

Ancient sand dunes are the building blocks of many of the earth's sedimentary rocks: sandstones laid down either by wind or water. Geologists have studied these rocks all around the globe. They peer back into the past, squinting through microscopes at grain patterns, aligning their Brunton compasses with various angles of deposition, holding up measuring rods to calculate thicknesses of bedding. But the best instrument for studying the past is a sound

understanding of processes operating in the present. For years, White Sands has offered geologists a perfect opportunity to study sand in the process of being deposited.

Geologist Edwin McKee's work amidst the dunes at White Sands in the 1960s and 1970s will always stand as a prime example of thoroughness and ingenuity in the study of sands and sandstone. McKee drilled, troweled, and bulldozed his way through the dunes. He mapped the monument on foot and from the air. He measured wind, rain, and temperatures round the clock and through the years. He made latex peels of dune surfaces that showed every conceivable internal angle of sand deposition. He sieved sand until he was blue in the face. And he began to understand how sand dunes are put together, how they work.

Sand grains can bounce across a dune surface in a wind-driven motion called *saltation*. Saltating grains usually rise no more than a few inches above the ground. If a grain is too heavy to be plucked by the wind from the ground, it can be nudged along by momentum imparted when an incoming saltating grain strikes the surface. This type of motion is called *creep*. Saltation generally accounts for 75 percent of wind-driven sand movement across a dune's surface, with the balance occurring as creep.

The amount of sand moved by the wind is a cubed function of wind velocity. In other words, a strong wind will carry a lot of sand, but a stronger wind will carry *a whole lot* of sand. Very little sand will be moved across the dunes unless

Dr. Edwin McKee at White Sands research site.

Wind-propelled sand grains nudge other grains as they bounce along the dune surface. Fine dust particles may float in the air.

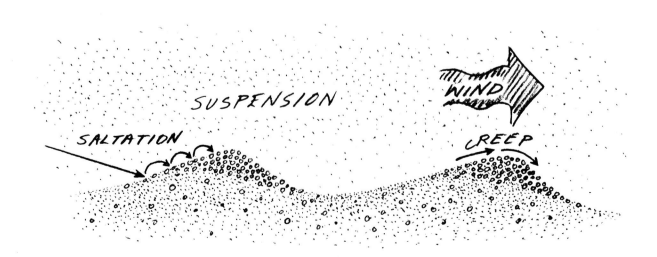

SUSPENSION

WIND

SALTATION

CREEP

Aerial photograph showing dunes and interdunes with a large pedestal held together by the roots of the plant atop it.

the wind is blowing at least fifteen miles an hour. But as wind speed rises above this threshold, a great deal of sand can be transported across a dune in short order. If the wind is blowing hard enough, sand grains can actually be "suspended" in the air, neither creeping nor saltating across a dune, but carried aloft. Dust particles are lighter and more likely to achieve suspension than sand grains.

Sand will accumulate into sheets and dunes when there is an adequate supply of sand and a wind of sufficient strength. At White Sands, McKee measured sand accumulating at a rate of two vertical inches per hour during winds that varied from seventeen to forty miles an hour.

But why does it accumulate in one place rather than another? Factors favoring local accumulation include proximity to source and a predictable and localized decrease in wind strength. Such a decrease in wind can occur behind an obstacle—be it a mountain range, a line of vegetation, or even a small rock. Saltating grains actu-

ally absorb a great deal of the wind's energy, thus slowing the wind near the ground. Consequently, the very presence of dune sand will locally decelerate the wind and encourage deposition of more sand.

Dunes have two basic faces: windward and lee. The windward slope gently rises in a downwind direction. Sand grains climb this surface either by saltation or creep. As a dune gains height relative to its neighbors, the top is less sheltered as it protrudes into stronger and stronger winds. At some point, the benefit of strong winds carrying more sand will be outweighed by the tendency of that strong wind to erode sand that would otherwise have been deposited at the top of the dune. The sand just bounces on over to the lee side of the dune. Unlike the gentle three- to ten-degree slope of the dune's windward side, the lee side slants down at about thirty-four degrees, the angle of repose of sand. Pile dry sand any steeper, and it will just slip downhill. Logically, the lee side is called the slipface of the dune. Depending on the amount of moisture present, sand will avalanche down this slipface either in an intact block called a *slump*, or in a free-for-all called *grainflow* where each sand grain moves independent of its neighbors.

So sand travels across a dune field by combinations of saltation and creep *up* the windward slope, and slumping and grainflow *down* the slipface. The grains move in response first to wind, then to gravity.

But more than just sand is moving across the field; entire dunes are moving too. It is as if, in a strong wind, each dune were picking up its petticoats, dancing a few steps downwind, and then settling back to earth when the music of the wind dies. As a dune moves downwind, it first covers then uncovers a given area. The area uncovered between dunes is called an *interdune*. In some places at White Sands National Monument, where the dunes are spread out because sand supply is diminished, interdunes are found in relative abundance. At other places, sand is more plentiful and the dunes crowd each other, burying some potential interdune areas.

McKee described four major types of dunes at White Sands. Each is found in particular areas of the monument. *Dome-shaped*, or embryonic, dunes grow close to the gypsum source at Lake Lucero. They are low, streamlined dunes that hold the White Sands Dune-speed Record. Dome-shaped dunes have been clocked at velocities approaching thirty-eight feet a year.

Barchan dunes assume a classic crescent shape: they have an upwind nose, with two downwind horns embracing a central slipface. The name is fittingly derived from the Arabic word for a ram's horn. Barchans can grow to a height of sixty-five feet at White Sands National Monument. Barchans tend to grow in areas with a somewhat limited supply of sand. As the amount of sand increases, these dunes grade into the third type, called *transverse* dunes. Like barchans, these have a rising windward slope and a more steeply slanting slipface. But rather than

The four types of dunes found at White Sands: dome-shaped, barchan, transverse, and parabolic.

Dome-shaped Dunes

Barchan Dunes

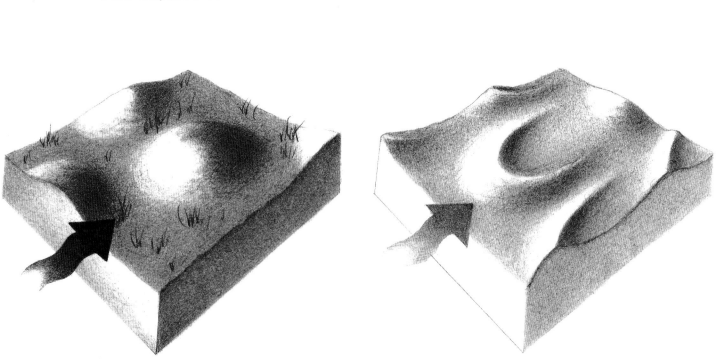

having arms that trail downwind, transverse dunes are continuous ridges of sand that lie perpendicular to the dominant wind. Both barchan and transverse dunes can move about twelve or thirteen feet a year at White Sands.

The final major dune type here is the *parabolic* dune. Like barchans, a parabolic dune has arms, but these extend upwind rather than down. The arms are anchored in place by vegetation, while the more mobile center of the dune continues to move downwind. Parabolic dunes are found on the downwind margins of the White Sands dune field, especially along the eastern border of the monument. These dunes move slowly, at rates of only two to eight feet per year; the slowest parabolic dunes are found right on the edges of the dune field.

Ripples are dune surface textures that are not only visually appealing, but also scientifically significant. Ripples can form when saltating grains encounter a slight unevenness on the surface over which they bounce. Incoming grains tend to

strike the upwind surface of a bump that projects up into their path. The grains are most likely to accumulate where they strike. Also, the landing grains will cause other grains to creep slightly uphill. Saltating grains tend to have a very shallow trajectory; they usually arrive at an angle of about ten degrees above horizontal. Consequently, the growing surface unevenness will cast a sort of saltation shadow across its own downwind side. Few saltating grains will land here. The distance between ripples (their "wavelength") tends to increase with wind speed, at least up to the point that the wind becomes so strong that it begins to destroy the ripple pattern all together.

Most geologic processes are ponderously slow: ancient seas come in, not-quite-so-ancient seas go out. The dunes of White Sands are remarkably young and nimble by comparison. Considered in a geologic time frame, they seem to zoom across the Tularosa Basin like little cars on a race track. When you walk in the dunes, it is easy to find signs of their passage. On the downwind edge of

Transverse Dunes

Parabolic Dunes

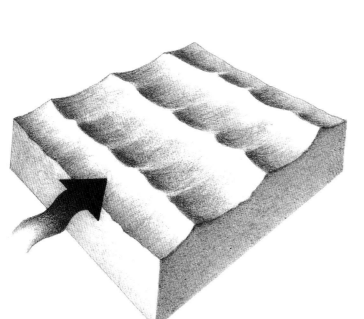

Curved ridges, formed when groundwater lightly cements sand grains together, are exposed when the rest of the dune blows away.

Ripple pattern created by wind-blown sand.

an interdune area, you will frequently see the graceful curving remnants of a previous dune. These curves are commonly preserved slipface bases, cemented during groundwater evaporation as the rest of a dune blows away. During the time that a dune exists within the dune field, rain water will percolate down from the top, and ground water may circulate up from the bottom. This water (especially the groundwater) carries minute quantities of dissolved gypsum which can precipitate into the spaces between individual grains, and the grains will be lightly cemented into place. Such cementation will happen most predictably at the bottom of the dune. And this cementation is likely to make the lowest layers more resistant to wind erosion.

Geologists have spent a lot of time trying to figure out the patterns in which the dunes move at White Sands. Eddie McKee was convinced that the dunes rode up over one another,

with the arrival of each new dune burying its predecessors a little bit deeper. His drilling in the dunes revealed that the sands average only thirty feet in thickness. Since McKee worked at White Sands, other geologists have gone on to suggest that buried dunes are amalgamated into the underlying interdune deposits, and do not retain their identity as individual dunes. These scientists have traced layers of silty sand across the dune field, concluding that these layers represent periods of widespread erosion during times when the supply of gypsum sand was depleted. They describe alternating periods of erosion and deposition of dunes at White Sands. Each period

could take at least five thousand years to blow through. Because they found evidence for two sequences of erosion and deposition, they concluded that dunes could have been present in the Tularosa Basin twenty thousand years ago.

Twenty thousand years might seem like a long time, but it is necessary to put that into perspective. Let's suppose our friendly neighborhood geologist wanted to make a home movie that showed the entire history of Mother Earth in two hours. The projector rolls at thirty frames a second. The geologist would have to adjust the camera so that each frame would span twenty thousand years. Deposition of the Yeso Formation would flicker onto the screen one hour and fifty-four minutes into the film, long after the popcorn was gone. The Tularosa Basin would form seventeen seconds before the end of the movie. And the sand dunes themselves would be created during the very last frame of the movie.

Desert within a Desert

he dunes at White Sands are often likened to a sand sea. But it may be more accurate to think of them as a desert within a desert, where unique conditions have produced plant and animal associations quite different from those in the Chihuahuan Desert region surrounding it.

To see the Chihuahuan Desert, you must travel to the borderlands of Arizona, New Mexico, and west Texas. As its name implies, the Chihuahuan Desert really belongs to Mexico. Only a small northern portion of it is found in the United States, where it crosses

The Chihuahuan is the largest of the North American deserts. Most of it lies within Mexico.

two dominant mountain ranges, the Sierra Madre Occidental and Oriental. A corridor of Chihuahuan Desert extends north into southeast Arizona, with an eastern lobe into southern New Mexico, in which squarely sits White Sands National Monument.

How do you know when you're in the Chihuahuan Desert? One way is to look at the vegetation: "indicator" species include soaptree yuccas that spear the blue sky, American tarbush on the mesas and slopes, the shin-damaging lechuguilla, the waxy candelilla, resinous creosote bush, lacy honey mesquite, and several kinds of grasses. Some, but not all, of these live in the unique environment of White Sands.

The Chihuahuan is not as lush, botanically, as the Sonoran Desert to the west. The main reason is that the Chihuahuan Desert receives about 70 percent of each year's rainfall in a single season: summer. Of White Sands' total average annual precipitation of nearly 8 inches, 4.8 inches arrive between July and September. The Sonoran Desert, because of its geographic position, receives both winter and summer rains, which nurture richer botanical diversity.

The Chihuahuan Desert waffles between desert and grassland, depending upon rainfall and slight soil variations. In dry periods, desert wins; in wet times, grasslands prevail. This dynamic situation is especially dramatic on the desert's northern edge.

over in blithe disregard of the chain link fence that defines the international border.

The edges of the Chihuahuan Desert are fuzzy. At least a dozen maps show a dozen different boundaries for this, the largest of the four great North American deserts. Nearly 90 percent of the Chihuahuan's more than two hundred thousand square miles is located in Mexico. Its heart is the high central plateau between Mexico's

Chihuahuan desertscrub typically includes creosote bush, prickly pear cactus, lechuguilla, and soaptree yucca. Ocotillo is also shown in this area near Big Bend National Park.

By geologic standards, the Chihuahuan Desert is fairly recent. It developed with the other three major southwestern deserts between eight thousand and four thousand years ago, only after the chilly and relatively wet Pleistocene had closed up shop. During the late Pleistocene, or ice age, sand dunes may have been part of the landscape but the plant life looked entirely different. Most of what is now a shrubby, grassy desert was a woodland of pinyon pine, oak, and juniper. A glacier capped Sierra Blanca, the isolated, twelve-thousand-foot peak that graces the distant skyline to the north of the park. Large, plant-eating mammals such as camels, horses, mammoths, and ground sloths roamed the ice-age woodlands. Signs of their passage remain in the form of inverted trackways preserved on gypsum pedestals on Alkali Flat, just north of Lake Lucero. In dry lake beds and in caves elsewhere in the Chihuahuan Desert, bones of these now-extinct large mammals have been found, along with the bones of voles and tiger salamanders, pinyon pine pollen, and the dung of ground sloths deposited eleven and twelve thousand years ago.

Soaptree yucca seedpod.

Radiocarbon dates obtained from this material show that by eleven thousand years ago, at the end of the Pleistocene, the region's climate began to change. Winter precipitation decreased, and the modern summer rainfall pattern of the Chihuahuan Desert emerged. Pinyons were no longer present in the woodland. The year-round lakes such as Lake Otero began to evaporate. The large grazers became extinct, possibly due to climate change or overhunting by people who were entering this part of the Southwest.

By eight thousand years ago, the oak and juniper woodland had retreated to higher elevations, and a desert grassland ecosystem had evolved. Finally, about four thousand years ago,

Lake Otero had completely evaporated, leaving the dry playa now known as Lake Lucero. The Chihuahuan desertscrub—the mesquite, creosote bush, and tarbush seen today in southern New Mexico—was established. And sitting at its northern edge were 275 square miles of gypsum dunes, the white sands.

On an afternoon late in September, the light is soft, the air clean and delicious. Long blue shadows stretch across the sand dunes. A gentle breeze rustles the dry brown capsules hanging from a bleached yucca stem. The capsules have split open, scattering black seeds onto the white sand. Each seed is about the size of a dime and as light as a slip of paper. Inside the six chambers of a capsule, more seeds are arranged in tightly packed clusters. At the base of the yucca, spiky green leaves spiral out of the sand.

Soaptree yuccas, marching across the dunes, are among the largest and most obvious plants that grow in the white sands. Otherwise, the desert lives up to classic first impressions: mile after mile of barren sand with nary a drop of water fit to drink. But the yucca manages to survive here, and, upon closer examination, so do many other plants and animals. Ripples on the dune surfaces are embroidered with the tracks of mice, lizards, and beetles. A smoky puff of shrub graces the crest of the next dune over. Far in the distance is a plant that looks large enough to be a tree.

No one said it was going to be easy. Plants and animals of White Sands must cope with scarce rainfall delivered in uneven amounts, soils poor in nutrients, swift changes in day and night temperatures, and scorching heat in summer. But creatures in deserts everywhere must meet similar conditions. What is unique, and most important, in the white sands is that their homes constantly move. On a calm day in autumn, the dunes are silent and still; but return in springtime, when the wind blasts through from the southwest at fifty miles an hour, and the overriding force of this movement becomes convincingly clear.

In the words of author Ann Zwinger, there exists in the active dune area a "continual tango between plant and blowing sand." And only a handful of plants can join in that dance. Take the widely distributed and successful yucca. As dunes sweep over a yucca plant, it elongates its stem, or trunk, to overcome burial and to keep its leaves above the sand so they can continue to

Flowering structures on Mormon tea.

photosynthesize. This rapid elongation of stems is a major adaptation not only of yucca but also of other successful dune plants. Yuccas also produce what are called *adventitious* roots, spidery appendages that grow along the stem. For young yuccas, these roots anchor the plant in its mobile home, and, as do all roots, transport water and nutrients to the plant. Because the adventitious roots are close to the surface, they also provide oxygen, crucial to the plant's growth.

Should seeds not find suitable soil for germination or should young seedlings be buried too quickly by sand, yuccas can draw on a backup reproductive system. New yucca plants can sprout from horizontal, underground stems called rhizomes, thus reproducing vegetatively. Yucca also appears able to switch to a faster metabolism to meet the rapidly changing dune environment.

Another survivor is the lovely, soft gray shrub called hoary rosemarymint. The shrub's common name tells of its membership in the mint family; the fragrance of a crushed leaf verifies this. Rosemarymint is one of the few plants whose seeds can germinate on the crests of the most active dunes. The silvery hairs that cover its leaves and stems prevent the plant from drying out in this arid environment.

Other lifeforms have met the challenges of the dunes in remarkable ways. The roots of the sticklike shrub called Mormon tea capture sand, forming mounds or hummocks around itself. The plants can grow through the hummocks, and, with the tight mass of roots and underground stems the hummock forms, the plants are anchored against even gale-force winds.

YUCCA AND MOTH

The relationship between the yucca and a moth is one of nature's most beautiful, and exclusive, symbiotic relationships. In White Sands, soaptree yuccas bear lovely creamy blossoms in late spring. (These waxy flowers show the yucca's kinship with the lily family.) In the evenings, the female pronuba moth visits the flowers. As this tiny moth moves from flower to flower, she gathers pollen, which she carries in a ball under her head. In the ovary of one yucca flower, she will lay eggs and, as she moves about, will also deposit the pollen onto the sticky stigma of that same flower.

Pronuba moth in yucca blossom.

But the story doesn't stop here. Because of the pronuba moth's pollination services, the yucca will flower and bear fruit and seeds, which the moth larvae will feed on when they emerge from the eggs. The larvae then bore their way out of the capsule and fall into the sand, where they overwinter, emerging in spring as adult moths. In this amazing example of coevolution, the pronuba moth has become the yucca's only pollinator, while yucca is the only plant that sustains the moth.

And though pronuba moths enjoy a highly specific relationship with the yucca, other insects frequent the plant as well. Sixty-seven different insect species have been noted on a single soaptree yucca in White Sands. Their casual contact does not lead to pollination because they may be too small or they do not come into contact with the stigma of the plant.

Sumac on pedestal.

browse the leaves and build nests and burrows in the shady, cool base of the sumac. Birds eat the red, citric berries.

Hoary rosemarymint routinely forms pedestals too. Cottonwood trees occasionally do, and yuccas as well, if several are growing together in a cluster. In some parts of White Sands, pedestals attain the size of small houses. Although the cemented pedestals will often outlast the plants they once supported, eventually, as has happened with Big Pedestal, near Point of Sands on the main highway south of the visitor center, they erode away. Little is permanent in the world of the white sands.

Even with all the factors working against them, trees do manage to live among the active dunes at White Sands National Monument. Rio Grande cottonwoods, known best for the thick groves, or *bosques*, they form along the floodplains of southwestern rivers, do grow here. Although they appear stunted because much of their trunks are buried by sand, cottonwoods in the white sands actually attain impressive heights. Their golden, leathery leaves in autumn are one of the few signs of changing seasons in this neutral landscape, and the accumulation of the leaves around the base of cottonwood trees provides a significant source of organic material for the impoverished soil.

A few plants form large pedestals of sand. One dramatic example of a pedestal-builder at White Sands is skunkbush sumac, also called squawbush. These shrubs bind gypsum grains into a compact mass around their tangled roots, branches, and trunk. When the sand blows away, or deflates, the plant stays put, "wrapped in a root-bound plaster cast," in the words of one naturalist. Sumac grows on top of pedestals and spills over them like a mane of dark, shaggy hair. These shrubs provide habitat, shelter, and food for many White Sands creatures as well. Wildlife

Rosemarymint flowers.

Cottonwoods show many of the same strategies as other dune plants to the coming and going of sand: elongated trunks, adventitious roots, and pedestal formation. The adventitious roots near the surface keep the trees' deeper roots fed with oxygen; otherwise they would suffocate.

The presence of cottonwoods signals the presence of water, for these trees need a continuous supply of water low in salinity. In White Sands, they grow roughly in a line stretching from northeast to southwest, a distribution possibly restricted and determined by groundwater supplies. One researcher has suggested that subsurface flow between Lost River in the northeast corner of the monument and Lake Lucero in the southwest corner may be the source of that water.

Besides the constant movement of their homes, plants in the white sands face another

Gyp nama.

predicament. Because of the high gypsum content of the soil, and lack of basic nutrients needed for growth, many plants do poorly here. Some, however, not only tolerate gypsum but actually demand it. Why certain species must have gypsum is not known. One suspicion is that they require high amounts of sulfates or sulphur, with which gypsum is certainly well endowed. These *gypsophilous* plants, as they are called, are ones found in the dune fields. Their common names— gyp moonpod, gyp nama, and gyp grama—speak of their highly specific propensities. Gyp moonpod, a perennial member of the four-o' clock family, grows on gypsum hills and at the edge of salt flats. Gyp nama is a strange, low-growing,

succulent-looking plant of the waterleaf family. Gyp grama is a native tufted grass. A shrub called frankenia, or mockheather, is another plant often associated with gypsum. The small white flowers on this one- or two-foot-tall shrub possess a unique structure: four-clawed petals and five stamens and five sepals united into a tube.

Other dune plants, such as yucca and four-wing saltbush, deal with their nutrient-poor environment by having special fungi growing on their roots. These fungi, called *mycorrhizae*, literally "mushroom roots," evolved in close association with their host plants. The fungi grow as a sheath around the plant's roots which helps the plant obtain water and nutrients. Meanwhile, the plant provides sugars and other foods for the fungi.

Because there is not a great deal of decaying organic material supplying nitrogen, it is one nutrient in high demand among dune plants. In an arrangement similar to mycorrhizal roots, bacteria grow on the roots of some plants, such as Indian ricegrass and members of the legume, or pea, family. The bacteria perform a good deed by changing nitrogen from the air into a form that plants can use in the sand. The plant reciprocates by supplying energy to sustain the bacteria.

One thing the soils of the white sands do not lack is salts. Salts present problems for plants because they keep them from pulling water from the soil. Some plants, called *halophytes*, have evolved adaptations that allow them to live in saline environments. A common White Sands plant, four-wing saltbush, is an example. The leaves of four-wing saltbush have special bladders that help the plant regulate salt concentrations. The bladders hold salts, like reservoirs; they finally swell and break open, depositing salt on the leaves. The saltiness of saltbush is noticeable in the taste of the plant's papery winged seeds.

Between the dunes are low, flat swales called interdunes. Just beneath the surface of an interdune is a band with a distinct green tinge. The source of the color is *cyanobacteria*, or blue-green algae. The cyanobacteria take nitrogen from the atmosphere and make it available for interdune plants. (Research has shown that these cyanobacteria may be heat lovers: their optimum growing temperature is 104 degrees Fahrenheit.)In association with fungi, these form a nubbly lichen crust that protects the surface of the interdunes from erosion. That crust, only about a quarter of an inch thick, is extremely fragile. A boot print here may still be visible five years hence, and the tire tracks of a vehicle can be seen a decade later. When walking in the dunes, it is preferable to stay at the edge between the interdune and active dune to avoid crushing the valuable crust.

This lichen crust must be present to stabilize the surface before plants can move in. On the damp, level ground of interdunes, seeds have a better chance of germinating. Golden clumps of grasses—alkali sacaton, little bluestem, Indian ricegrass, and sandhill muhly—dot the interdunes like shocks of wheat. Interdunes are destined to be covered by the constantly moving dunes, but while these spaces are open, plants arrive in a sequence that follows a fairly clear pattern, at least on interdunes among the parabolic dunes: white evening primrose is the pioneer plant, followed quickly by sandhill muhly, practically a symbol of the interdunes. Little bluestem and some large clumps of

Close-up view of interdune surface.

Climax stage interdune vegetation with flowering rabbitbrush.

sandhill muhly characterize the next stage; then blue grama takes over to form a nearly continuous cover. The "climax" stage, reached at the oldest part of the interdune (the part farthest from the encroaching active dune), includes purple bursage and shrubs like Mormon tea, rabbitbrush, and four-wing saltbush. Eventually, an encroaching dune moves across the interdune, destroying those plants in its path that cannot withstand burial. A new interdune is created elsewhere, and the pattern starts again.

The cyanobacteria of the fragile interdune crust do more than provide firm footing for plants. They also feed a host of tiny mites that live in the soil and in the leaves and plant litter that accumulate under shrubs. Other mites graze on fungi and then transport the fungal spores to places where they will grow. The mites and small soil organisms perform yeoman service in the dunes, going about their invisible business of decomposing plant matter and recycling it into the ecosystem. By all accounts, these diminutive creatures do an admirable job. Decomposition rates, though expected to be low in this desert, are surprisingly fast at White Sands, on the order of decomposition rates in the much moister tropics.

The dampness often characteristic of interdunes is explained by the fact that the water table is within a few feet of the surface in White Sands. At least one interdune plant has taken advantage of this favorable groundwater situation. Over most of its range, the low-growing sand verbena is an annual, blooming, setting seed, and completing its life cycle within the same season. It is a technique used by many warm-desert species in response to aridity. But in White Sands, sand verbena does something different: it becomes a perennial, overwintering and putting out its intoxicatingly fragrant, pale pink flowers again the following spring. The perennial lifestyle apparently is possible because of the moisture supplied by groundwater near the surface of the interdunes.

During winter and early spring, standing water sometimes collects in the interdune basins. Grasses and shrubs reflect in these mirrors, and migrating shorebirds, such as sandpipers and dowitchers, occasionally stop here.

On the Edges

T he farther east you go from the active dunes, the more plant life you will see. On the southern and eastern edges of the monument, extending two or three miles into the dune field, are the parabolic dunes. With their noses pointing forward and arms trailing behind, parabolic dunes are the reverse shape of the active barchan dunes.

Familiar shrubs of the active dunes—including skunkbush sumac, rosemarymint, and rabbitbrush—are here too, but in greater numbers. The plants anchor the arms of parabolic dunes, while the noses of the dunes push on like freighters through the ocean.

Large grassy areas separate the parabolic dunes, and saltbush rings the outside margin of the stable dune area. Because of the increased plant life, wildlife find more shelter and food among the stable dunes. There are more quail, pocket mice, and coyotes than in the restless, active dune field.

The parabolic dunes on the margin of the monument aren't going anywhere fast; the plants have done too good a job slowing them down. Some of the marginal dunes are creeping forward

Claretcup cactus amid four-wing saltbush.

only inches each year, compared to thirty-eight feet of yearly progression for the more mobile dunes. Did the plants finally stop the wayward dunes? Or, did the dunes stop for some other reason and the plants then take advantage of a stable situation? It is a chicken-and-egg question, because each process reinforces the other.

Slow-growing plants such as saltbushes, buffalo gourds, and cacti fare much better in the stable dune area. In exchange for their proficiency at saving water, cacti grow very slowly. Some sixteen cactus species have been identified within the national monument. The life history of one, the claretcup, is well known from detailed studies in White Sands.

Three separate claretcup populations, numbering more than 250 individual plants, have been located and observed in White Sands. Biologists found that it takes about twenty-seven years for a single claretcup stem to reach a maximum length of twenty inches, with growth averaging less than an inch a year. These cacti reach huge sizes; old individuals grow up to five feet in diameter with seventy-five stems. In late spring, claretcup blooms with the gorgeous crimson chalices that give the plant its name. Some two hundred flowers have been counted on one spectacular individual in White Sands! All three life stages of claretcup—seedling, intermediate, and old-aged ones—can be found together. This suggests that each population started from a single cactus which produced seeds that germinated close by. Ants, rodents, rabbits, wind, and rain are the agents that help disperse the cactus seeds.

Throughout its long and vigorous life, a claretcup is associated with another plant, saltbush. Saltbush acts as a "nurse" plant; moist moss beneath it provides an ideal germination bed for the cactus seeds. Once a claretcup germinates, the seedling is shaded by the shrub. In the microenvironment beneath the saltbush, soil temperatures can be forty degrees cooler than in open, sunny areas nearby. Nevertheless, many cactus seedlings still die from desiccation during long, dry periods.

Those claretcups that survive do not show proper gratitude to their nurse plants. Trying always to be the first to soak up moisture in the topmost layer of soil, the claretcup sends out shallow, fibrous roots that compete with those of saltbush. Finally, the cactus excludes its nurse plant by changing the soil conditions and deflecting its stem. This habit seems to be widespread: 80 percent of claretcups on three sites in White Sands were growing next to dead saltbush plants.

When a claretcup reaches reproductive age, jackrabbits and cottontails feed on the juicy red fruits, and rodents eat the roots and green tissue. Eventually, fungi and ants invade the cactus, and woodrats burrow into crevices. Woodrats probably favor the even day-to-night temperatures they find under the cactus. Their burrowings, however, sever the plant's roots and will kill the cactus.

The long-lived claret-cups can also die of one other thing—old age.

The rugged San Andres Mountains are mirrored in the clear waters of Lake Lucero. This is a rare sight, water in this lake, for Lucero is a *playa*, to the Spaniards a "beach," to geologists a normally dry lake bed. Most of the time Lucero *is* dry, its surface broken into glossy curls of parched mud. But in wet years the lake holds

Lake Lucero.

several feet of salty, gypsum-laden brew, mostly groundwater that must rise only a few feet to reach the surface.

Lake Lucero can be visited only with a park ranger, for the road that leads to Lucero crosses the White Sands Missile Range. Many people choose to make the pilgrimage, however, because Lake Lucero answers one of the most often-asked questions in White Sands: "Where does the sand come from?"

The lake is located at the far western edge of the national monument, in the shadow of the San Andres Mountains. The path to the lakeshore follows an arroyo lined with mesquite and tarbush. Along the way pieces of selenite, a crystal form of gypsum, protrude from the streambanks like sherds of glass. People stoop for closer examination of this sparkling mineral that contributes to the dunes of white sand.

Gooey, ankle-deep muck lines the edges of the lake, making it difficult for a person to approach and dabble a toe in the water. The only plant that can tolerate the alkaline soils of the lakeshore is pickle-weed, a relative of saltbush. This succulent, evergreen-looking plant is also called iodinebush and *hierba del burro*. Some animals do manage to live in the sediments

Anthill in interdune area.

of Lake Lucero; more than twenty species of protozoa, bacteria, algae, nematodes, and brine shrimp have been identified. One is a purple sulfur bacteria that "blooms," or multiplies, usually in fall, giving the lake a distinctly rosy hue. When there is water, a few beetles and aquatic insects have been seen in Lucero as well.

To the north of Lake Lucero is a shimmering vacant expanse called Alkali Flat, an improbably level and impossibly barren land—164 square miles stretching north from Lake Lucero along the western boundary of the dune field—part of the lakebed of the ice-age Lake Otero. There truly is almost no life on the flat, except ants. Large numbers of harvester ants forage at sunrise and in late afternoon if clouds conceal the sun. With few seeds to eat on Alkali Flat, the ants must wait for insects to settle to the ground at night or for the wind to carry in plant material. The ants dredge, sort, and cover their hills with a neat mosaic of tiny black rocks and ladybird beetle parts. Their huge, evenly spaced mounds provide the only relief to this otherwise surreal place.

Foothill slopes, or *bajadas*, sweep grandly down from the San Andres Mountains into the valley. The bajadas are cut by shallow arroyos and dotted with grassy meadows. On these slopes grow plants more characteristic of the Chihuahuan Desert, such as creosote bush, known in Spanish as *gobernador* and *hediondilla*, or "little stinker." This name comes from its memorable smell after a rain, a heady, resinous odor that fills the atmosphere. Grazing and browsing animals shun the olive-green leaves of creosote bush

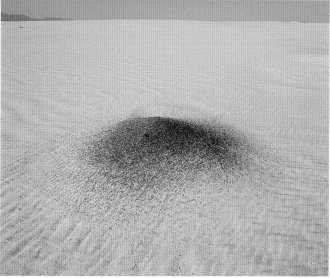

because of the resins they contain; but Native Americans found it a veritable grocery and pharmacy. Various concoctions of the plant were believed to cure everything from worms, to syphilis, to chest ailments. This successful shrub moved into the Southwest in post-Pleistocene times, when arid conditions began to hold sway. Creosote bushes may be among the oldest living plants, their venerability exceeding even that of bristlecone pines.

Growing in a belt just below the creosote bush are honey mesquites. These, and the few scattered cottonwoods, are the only native trees found within the monument. Mesquite is the dominant member of this foothill plant association, along with other companions such as yucca, tumbleweed, saltbush, and a few grasses. Well known in southwestern deserts, mesquite has a substantial taproot that probes deeply for water. Its soft leaves lend welcome shade in the fierce heat of summer, but wicked thorns on the branches deter intruders.

Clockwise from top left:
Creosote bush.
Rio Grande cottonwood.
Cottonwood leaf.
White Sands mustard.
Sand verbena.

With denser plant life comes a correspondingly greater number of rodents, rabbits, mice, and squirrels. In turn, their presence encourages the appearance of larger mammals, such as coyotes, bobcats, and foxes on the bajadas and in the mountain canyons. The rugged canyons and cliffs of the San Andres provide excellent terrain for mountain lions. Because they harbor a sufficient population of mule deer and other animals, and because of their inaccessibility, these mountains have also been considered suitable habitat for reintroduction of the endangered Mexican wolf. Wolves, common in New Mexico in the early twentieth century, were killed off by vigorous government predator-control programs. Most wolves were gone by the 1940s; their last stronghold was in Hidalgo County, in the far southern part of the state. Only a remnant population remains in Chihuahua, Mexico.

Animals in White

What would you do if you were a lizard living in White Sands? No doubt, you would dress for the occasion. The advantage of color adaptation to an animal, whether in sand dunes or elsewhere, is to avoid being seen by predators. In this world of whiteness, there are some fascinating examples of color adaptation among members of the lizard community.

One example of color matching involves the Cowles prairie lizard, a subspecies of the western fence lizard, also called the White Sands swift. Normally a dark grayish-brown color, the Cowles subspecies is pale gray to nearly white in the active dune area. Here it has an immaculate white belly with bright blue patches on belly and throat.

Cowles lizards spend most of their time in the interdunes, among the rabbitbrush, yucca, ephedra, and Indian ricegrass. They are active throughout the day, but most are morning creatures, out between 9 a.m. and 11 a.m., basking under the branches of plants where some sun filters through. As the day wears on, they become inactive, almost never straying more than three feet away from the shade. Cowles lizards are real homebodies. Researchers captured and removed three from their homes beneath a rabbitbrush in White Sands, taking them three dunes and two depressions away. In only four days, all three had returned to that same shrub.

Because lizards are "cold-blooded" animals, that is, their body temperatures vary with those of their surroundings, they set their internal thermostats by moving from sun to shade. Lizards have other adaptations to the desert—impervious skins, excretion of nearly solid uric acid instead of urea, which requires water to dilute toxicity; and an ability to obtain moisture from their food.

Another sand-dwelling lizard is the bleached earless lizard, a white form of the lesser earless. Common on the dunes and interdunes, the bleached earless lizard (which does indeed lack ear openings) does not stay as close to plants as does the Cowles. It forages in open areas and is most active between 9 a.m. and noon. During the hottest hours of the afternoon, when soil temperatures can exceed 120 degrees Fahrenheit, the bleached earless lizard burrows into the sand. It reemerges in late day, as the soil starts to cool.

Male earless lizards vary in color from dark bluish-gray to nearly pure white, with dark and white spots on the back and sides of the body. In midmorning, males often assume positions on higher areas, near the base of a sand verbena or clump of ricegrass, and show challenge displays. During the breeding season in June, the males engage one another in biting, tail thrashing, pursuit, and bluff displays. In late June and early July, egg-carrying females often develop lemon-yellow to orange markings on their hind limbs, heads, and sides. By mid-July, they have deposited their eggs, and the bright markings begin to fade.

Preceding page:
Track of snake in sand.

Cowles prairie lizard or
White Sands swift.

Plains pocket mouse.

Little striped whiptail.

The little striped whiptail provides the third example of color adaptation among White Sands lizards. The normal whiptail is dark in color with bright-blue tail and throat. In the central dune area, however, they are much lighter, ranging from pale yellowish-gray to pale bluish-gray. Six or seven light stripes line their backs. Whiptails forage around plants but are also often out in direct sunlight. All summer the males fight with one another, and when the males try to follow females in July, the females turn and chase them.

Lizards aren't the only animals that exhibit color adaptation in White Sands. A mammal, the plains (or Apache) pocket mouse, is a blonde. Pocket mice are members of a distinctly southwestern rodent family classified between the true mice and the squirrels.

In White Sands the tiny plains pocket mouse, which weighs less than an ounce, has beady black eyes and yellow-tinged white fur with black-tipped guard hairs. All the other characteristics of this mouse, except color, match those of the same species living outside the dunes. The color of the plains pocket mouse in White Sands matches the sand so well that in daylight the ani-

mals are difficult to see, and at night nearly impossible. Their tracks are everywhere on the dunes each morning, evidence of their furtive nocturnal searches for rabbitbrush and grass seeds. They store seeds in their cheek pouches which, like those of kangaroo rats, their close kin, are fur-lined.

These animals' ability to change color hasn't happened on a moment's notice. The adaptation has evolved through countless generations of lizards and mice. As light-colored individuals successfully evaded predators, their genes were passed on and they were favored through natural selection to live in the sand dunes. The opposite color adaptation, incidentally, is seen among the malpais terrain in Valley of Fires (see page 12) north of White Sands. Here, lizards and mice are nearly black, all the better to hide among the tortured, dark basalt rocks of this volcanic region.

In White Sands, the most notable nemeses of lizards and mice are the dozen different kinds of snakes that live here. (Included are three rattlesnakes—prairie, western diamondback, and massasauga—often found curled up in clumps of grass.) Lizards must also beware of

Prairie rattlesnake.

Desert massasauga.

Camel cricket.

White grasshopper.

another predator, the loggerhead shrike. This bird, a summer resident in the northern Chihuahuan Desert, has been known to capture lizards and hold them in place by impaling them on the needle-sharp points of yucca leaves. This method of capture is necessary because shrikes lack talons with which to grasp the lizards.

Insects, which make up a large percentage of the life-forms in White Sands, also show color adaptations—including a nearly transparent camel cricket, and a grasshopper, a tiger beetle, and a snout beetle that have white forms. In stark contrast, darkling beetles are black as ravens. They are among the few insects active on the sands in midday. As one of these beetles tiptoes across the interdunes, past a tissue-white evening primrose and the bright pink flower of a centaury, it stops to investigate a sand verbena. Whenever it stops, the beetle assumes a characteristic posture—nose in sand, back end raised.

How does a black beetle survive in the desert? Under its hard wing covers is an insulative air pocket. The black color may also help the beetle absorb warmth in early morning, so it can become active before other insects and hold that warmth when nighttime temperatures dip precipitously. Likewise, they may be able to become more active earlier and later in the year.

White Sands animals have other ways of evading heat and staying warm. A burrow twelve inches into the sand experiences almost no temperature change throughout the day and is a good place to keep cool. In the economy of the desert, burrow-sharing appears to be common. Little striped whiptails have been found in the burrows of Cowles lizards, darkling beetles, pocket mice, and pocket gophers.

Small bulges on the surface of interdunes show evidence of the activity of the pocket gopher. Working alone, a gopher digs a main tunnel about four to six inches underground and constructs shallower side tunnels off the main one. It continuously backfills the tunnels, sealing the entrances to keep out badgers, coyotes, and foxes.

Though abundant in White Sands, pocket gophers are rarely seen because of their nocturnal lifestyle. They spend their days in the coolness of underground burrows, where they eat the roots and stems of perennial plants. When they come out at night, they gather grasses, which they cache in piles in their burrows.

These brown to blackish rat-sized rodents share with pocket mice and kangaroo rats the trait of fur-lined cheek pouches. The gophers' powerful front legs and long claws on the front feet make them incredibly efficient subterranean burrowers. Pocket gophers tunnel only where soils are suitable and usually avoid the sand dunes themselves. Thus, the interdune gopher populations may be isolated from one another. Described as "cantankerous" animals, pocket gophers generally lead solitary existences except during breeding season.

The burrows of kit foxes have also been found in the gypsum pedestals or mounds. Often, they excavate several openings where the branches of plants hang down to cover them. A park ranger who observed kit fox families in the dunes in late June noted that the young kits normally emerged from the den just before sunset and reentered the den by 8:30 in the morning. Graceful hunters, kit foxes pounce on mice, gophers, and rabbits. At one White Sands den, jackrabbit carcasses were consumed. At a den near a backcountry campsite, remains of a bleached lizard, a centipede, and a package of breakfast rolls were found.

Of all the things you might *not* expect to find in White Sands, one would be a flowing river and the other would be a desert fish. But in this place of extremes and surprises, there is a river, with a very special fish to go with it. It is, literally, the Lost River, an ephemeral stream that crosses the northeast edge of the monument. Originating in an area drained by Malone Draw north of Holloman Air Force Base, Lost River flows into White Sands National Monument in a defined channel. But its life is short; it soon wanders in several braided channels and is absorbed into a dry lake.

Lost River is significant because it often contains standing water which, like water in deserts everywhere, attracts all kinds of animals. Signs of badger, coyote, kit fox, skunk, gopher, and kangaroo rat have all been seen at Lost River. Also, a good population of a rare plant called sea-lavender grows along the riverbed.

In the waters of Lost River have been found a two-inch, silvery-gray fish with a protruding jaw called the White Sands pupfish. Pupfishes are products of the Pleistocene, when the large lakes dried up and left them physically and genetically

ORYX

On a walk through the dunes, you will likely notice large, heart-shaped tracks obviously made by a hoofed animal. There is a good chance you will also see the animal that made the tracks—the oryx. This antelope, also called a gemsbok, is a native of sub-Sahara Africa where it reaches greatest concentrations among the sand dunes of the Kalahari Desert.

The New Mexico Department of Game and Fish first introduced oryx into the White Sands Missile Range in 1969 as a game animal. Oryx have since roamed into the national monument and established home ranges here. The ninety-eight animals introduced between 1969 and 1977 have reproduced so successfully that their numbers have reached as high as twelve hundred individuals.

Oryx are striking animals with long, straight horns and handsome black, cream, and gray coats. Although bulls may travel alone, oryx mostly move in herds. Cautious and alert, members of a herd watch anyone approaching on foot, circle around the newborn oryx, and sometimes make slight advances, called threat displays. Like most wild animals, they avoid people. Nevertheless, these animals may attack or injure people if threatened.

In midday, between active periods in morning and late afternoon, oryx seek shade wherever they find it—under shrubs or trees and even under culverts and beside power poles. Grasses are a favorite food, but they also eat plants, such as buffalo gourd and yucca, which provide moisture when free-standing water is unavailable. Oryx prefer open, grassy areas and interdunes, where they dig in the sand for water.

Vegetation in the national monument is showing the effects of oryx grazing, and the National Park Service has a general policy of eliminating nonnative animals. Hence, the park service plans to fence the monument's entire boundary to exclude these nonnative animals.

White Sands pupfish.

isolated. The White Sands pupfish has been observed in only a handful of places in the Tularosa Basin, Lost River being one, and it is the only fish native to the basin.

The pupfish prefers shallow pools and calm springs, oases in the desert. This highly adapted species tolerates conditions that are anathema to most aquatic creatures. It can withstand high levels of salinity and great daily fluctuations in water temperature. During their two- to three-year life span, pupfishes eat mosquito larvae, organic debris, aquatic insects, algae, and occasionally their own eggs and fry.

Their preference for mosquito larvae leads to the story of the discovery of the White Sands pupfish. The public health service was searching for a fish that ate mosquitoes, to control the numbers of these carriers of the virus that causes encephalitis. (An outbreak of encephalitis had hit Dona Ana County, New Mexico, where White Sands is located, in 1958.) They were looking, too, for a fish that could survive the extremes of desert waters. One man, who had run cattle across the Tularosa Basin in the 1920s, recalled a pond between White Sands and Valley of Fires where he had seen fish. In 1967, he took a health inspector to that pond. The fish collected there turned out to be the White Sands pupfish, which a scientist finally identified in 1975. It was named *Cyprinodon tularosa*.

In that same year the species was listed by the state of New Mexico as endangered. It is also a candidate for the federal threatened and endangered species list. Among threats to their existence are pollution, groundwater pumping that might take water from their ponds, and possible introduction of nonnative fish such as largemouth bass. Though White Sands pupfish are abundant in the few places they live, they are vulnerable

PORCUPINES

A most unlikely mammal lives in the cottonwoods in White Sands—the porcupine. Usually associated with snowy evergreen forests, these rodents appear to have adapted just fine, thank you, to the desert environs of White Sands.

Although the animals themselves may not often be seen, their signs are obvious, especially around cottonwoods. Porcupines eat the leaves and twigs of these trees, and when nothing else is available, the bark as well. In places, cottonwood branches are scraped clean where porcupines have eaten. As they waddle from tree to tree, porcupines leave telltale tracks with trailing drag marks, like big commas in the sand.

Predators are not a great concern to a porcupine: the thirty thousand barbed quills each animal possesses provide more than adequate deterrence. When threatened, the porcupine raises the quills "in the zoological equivalent of a cholla cactus," writes author Bil Gilbert. They do not, however, throw their quills. Instead, they slap their tails when threatened at close range.

Porcupines love salt; perhaps the highly saline soil and water of White Sands satisfies this essential need.

because one incident could wipe out the entire population in a given location. One pupfish population in a pond near Alamogordo was killed off in 1976 when its pond dried up. Feral horses on the White Sands Missile Range also present a problem. The horses frequent the ponds and springs where pupfish live, drinking and fouling the water and trampling the banks. Some of the springs are being fenced, and water is piped out for the horses. Meanwhile, a conservation plan has been drawn up to protect the pupfish and its habitat.

On more than one occasion, pupfish have been seen near and in Lost River in the national monument. Those fish likely were washed downstream during heavy rains. Biologists doubt that pupfish can survive the predictable drying up of Lost River in the monument. But pupfish have adapted to their fickle desert environment by producing many offspring, so they can afford substantial losses and still have enough stock to continue reproducing.

Lost River hosts not only a rare native fish, but also a notorious invading tree, the tamarisk. In the late 1970s, an estimated twenty thousand tamarisks, or salt cedars, were growing along Lost River within the national monument. The dense thickets of tamarisk along the river serve as a perpetual, large seed source for continued spread of this exotic species into the monument. Indeed, tamarisk is now widespread in White Sands—along Lake Lucero and Alkali Flat, at Big Pedestal, near park headquarters, and even in the interdunes and active dunes. Tamarisk seems able to withstand sand burial by elongating its stems, just as some native plants do. One biologist has called it the monument's "most serious plant threat."

Introduced in the 1850s as a windbreak and shade tree, this Mediterranean species now covers at least a million acres in fifteen western states. Tamarisk is notorious because it is such a successful invader. A single tree produces millions of tiny seeds that are scattered by the wind and that germinate in moist conditions. During floods on the Rio Grande in 1942-43, some twenty thousand acres were instantly occupied by "tammies." In White Sands, as elsewhere, tamarisks steal water from native plants, such as cattails, sedges, cottonwoods, and baccharis. (One tamarisk tree can soak up an estimated three hundred gallons of water a day.)

It has become clear to many people that tamarisk is probably here to stay. Though almost impossible to eradicate, it can be controlled to some extent. Methods are labor intensive and meet with varying success. In White Sands, volunteers have pulled tamarisk up by the roots and cut down larger ones. Significant regrowth occurs in a short time if the trees are only cut. A chemical can be applied to the stump to kill new sprouts, but use of chemicals in a national monument is not always acceptable. Uprooting saplings may prove a better technique to deter the spread of tamarisk.

Lizard tracks in sand.

The Frontier

Ten thousand years ago, on the shores of Lake Otero, hunters stalked bison and took them down with spears. The spears were armed with finely fluted stone points that the hunters sometimes left behind. Such points, which archeologists call "Folsom" type, have been found on the shorelines of playas in the Tularosa Basin. Here these nomadic hunters camped long enough to butcher the bison to feed their hungry families.

Although they may not have known it, these hunters were seeing the end of a major climatic period—the Pleistocene. About eight thousand years ago people lived by hunting big game as well. But by this time, they had to practice greater skill and search more diligently, for the large mammals were becoming more scarce as the grasslands gave way to desert. These people's tools, though similar to those of the earlier Folsom types, have often been found around ponds and seeps, a sign that the people were turning to these sources as the waters of the large lakes dwindled.

Folsom point replicas.

About seven thousand years ago, people had changed their lifestyles significantly. They still hunted, but for smaller animals, such as mule deer, pronghorn, and rabbits. They had also diversified, adding a wide repertoire of wild plants to their diet. The seasonal ripenings of various plants determined people's movements. In spring, fresh greens and sweet agave hearts brought welcome relief from monotonous winter foods. In late summer, cactus fruit and mesquite beans were ready to pick. In autumn, grass seeds and pinyon nuts were gathered.

From their mountain and foothill homes, these hunter-gatherers came into the valleys and the dunes to gather the seeds of Indian ricegrass, which ripen in late May, the earliest grasses to do so. The large, nutty-tasting seeds of ricegrass were plentiful and easy to harvest. Large amounts were carried from the desert valleys into mountain shelters where the seeds were winnowed and parched.

Ricegrass might also have been cooked in hearths found in White Sands, though archeologists have not yet excavated the sites to know for certain. Dozens of these hearths have been found, some more than ten feet across. Used repeatedly over thousands of years, the hearths formed gypsum pedestals, much like the pedestals formed by the roots and branches of the skunkbush sumac.

The hearth pedestals, formed not by nature but by humans, are distinctive. They contain blackened charcoal layers and are now plaster of paris, the product that results when gypsum is heated. Repeated rains have hardened and preserved the pedestals.

From six thousand to about two thousand years ago, the people of the Tularosa region continued their mobile, self-sufficient lives, traveling from basin floor to the mountains and back again to obtain plants and animals. But another great change was occurring among prehistoric people, the introduction of corn, or maize, probably brought north from Mexico. At a place called Fresnal Shelter, a rock alcove in the Sacramento Mountains east of Alamogordo, three-thousand-year-old corn was found, some of the oldest corn in the Southwest. But corn had not yet usurped the role of wild plants. Residents of Fresnal Shelter used more than thirty different native plants regularly.

By two thousand years ago, however, corn had become the number-one food group for prehistoric Tularosans. From a corn farmer's point of view, the Tularosa Basin has much in its favor. The frost-free growing season lasts more than two hundred days. Water is available at the mouths of mountain canyons, and half the year's precipitation comes during the summer growing season.

Growing corn meant settling down to tend the crop and store the surplus. Throughout the Southwest, a similar pattern was occurring at the time. People were digging pits in the ground, covering them with brush roofs, and calling them home. Family and friends often stayed together and built several of these pithouses next to one another, until they were living in villages. By A.D. 600 to 800, pithouse villages had been established at the mouths of canyons along the eastern edge of the Tularosa Basin.

Archeologists label the people of this time the Jornada Branch of the Mogollon culture, for the Mogollon Mountains west of White Sands near the New Mexico–Arizona border. The Mogollones also started to make pottery, a great technological advancement, for cooking and storing food. By this time, beans and squash had been added to the crop list.

By A.D. 1000, building construction methods became more elaborate. The Mogollon people started to erect above-ground masonry pueblos with many rooms. During this time, such pueblo villages surrounded by large fields were located on floodplains in the Tularosa Basin. A hundred years later, many people were living in two very large villages beside Lake Lucero.

By A.D. 1300 or 1350 all the major villages in the Tularosa Basin were vacated. Some people may have headed north to Gran Quivira on Chupadera Mesa, while others likely went to northern Mexico. Why they left after ten thousand years of successful adaptation in the region is a question archeologists are still trying to answer. The traditional explanation involves a long drought in the Southwest in the late 1200s that ended the agricultural cornucopia the people had enjoyed. More recent discussions, however, focus on changes in trade and social networks that may have led to the migrations.

Sierra Blanca, "White Mountain," is a landmark for travelers in the white sands. This twelve-thousand-foot peak, snowcapped most of the year, rises grandly on the northeastern horizon. Sierra Blanca was the heart of the homeland of another group of Native Americans who entered the region in the early 1500s. They were the Apaches, or Indeh. The Apaches were Southern Athapaskans, who along with their cousins, the Navajos, migrated south from western Canada. The exact date of the Apache arrival in southern New Mexico is uncertain, but several Spanish expeditioners chronicled the presence of Indians, probably Apache bands, in the 1580s living in grass huts or tents at the north end of the San Andres and along the Pecos River and Rio Grande.

The early history of the Apaches is murky, with many tribes and subdivisions bearing a bewildering variety of names. A general separation, however, was being made by the 1600s between those who hunted bison on the Plains and the southern nomads, who eventually became known as the Mescalero Apaches and whose territory included the huge land that stretched between the Pecos River on the east and the Rio Grande on the west. Although there is little record of their presence in the white sands proper, the Mescaleros lived in all the surrounding mountains—Organ, San Andres, and Sacramentos, as well as Sierra Blanca.

Hostilities were frequent between the Apaches, Spaniards, and Pueblo Indians at Gran Quivira and Pecos in the 1600s. The Apaches and Pueblos called truces long enough to trade with one another, the Apaches bartering buffalo hides, meat, horses, and slaves in exchange for crops and products grown and made by the Pueblos.

The Mescaleros were trapped, geographically, between Spanish troops moving eastward from the Rio Grande and the Comanches on the Plains. The Apaches, known for their fierceness as warriors, met their match in the Comanches. And despite an appeal for peace in 1770, the Apaches became the subjects of an all-out campaign by the Spaniards during the 1770s and 1780s.

Initially, the Apaches were hunter-gatherers, living much like the Archaic people had five thousand years earlier. Their diverse desert and mountain territory contained immense resources

San Juan, head chief of Mescalero Apache circa 1880.

that they knew where to obtain and how to prepare: agave, creosote bush, mesquite, yucca, prickly pear, grasses, juniper, pinyon, oak, ponderosa, fir, deer, pronghorn, rabbit, and prairie dogs.

They knew where all the water sources were, and their language closely describes available water: a playa lake where water remains for a brief period, one where water remains for a long time, a permanent lake, a spring that runs only after rains. Mescalero men and women also gathered salt from many of the dry lake beds in the white sands region. In August or September, when the lakes were usually dry, they traveled to these places and filled sack-shaped hides with salt.

From many of their mountain vantage points, the Mescaleros could see the shimmering white-ness of the sand dunes; only under duress would they try to cross the sands. Most of the time they took the mountain passes, such as San Augustin through the Organ Mountains to the south. The Mescalero Apaches did have a word for the white sands, *tse·hika*, and another, *tse·yahnka*, which meant the "lower edge of the sand," where one of their old trails crossed the southern boundary of the basin.

The tribe's name, *Mescalero*, means "mescal people." It is derived from their traditional reliance on the mescal or agave plant. In late spring, when the plant's fleshy stalks shoot up in a meteoric spurt of growth, Mescalero women set out for the foothills with hatchets and sticks to harvest and prepare the agave. The process lasted several days. First, they dug out the bulbs, or hearts, of the agave and placed them in a big cooking pit, properly blessed with prayers. The pit was covered with generous amounts of dampened grass, dirt, and rocks. The agave hearts were steamed a full day and night. The sticky, sweet morsels were then pulled from the pit and eaten with delight.

Agave with stalk.

The year 1846 marks the beginning of the end of the traditional Apache way of life. There was a brief period of relative stability between 1856 and 1858, when Indian Agent Michael Steck set up some Apaches on farms at the mouth of La Luz and Alamo canyons near Alamogordo.

But these well-meaning attempts were erased by the entry of United States Army General James Henry Carleton. Confident and inflexible, Carleton believed the only solution to the "Indian problem" was to sequester the Apaches on a reservation and convert them into Christian

Kit Carson.

farmers. In 1862, he sent orders to his field commander, Colonel Christopher Carson, that "All Indian men of that tribe are to be killed whenever and wherever you find them. The women and children will not be harmed, but you will take them prisoners."

A band of five hundred Mescalero Apaches was the first to be attacked in Dog Canyon at the south end of the Sacramentos. Those who survived, including Chief Cadete, actually went to Carson for protection. Cadete said: "You have driven us from our last and best stronghold, and we have no more heart. Do with us as may seem good to you, but do not forget we are men and braves."

General Carleton then ordered the Mescaleros to Bosque Redondo, or Fort Sumner, a reservation on the Pecos River in east-central New Mexico. Those who refused to go or who tried to hide, as some did, were to be killed. But the majority of the Apaches went to Bosque Redondo, and by the

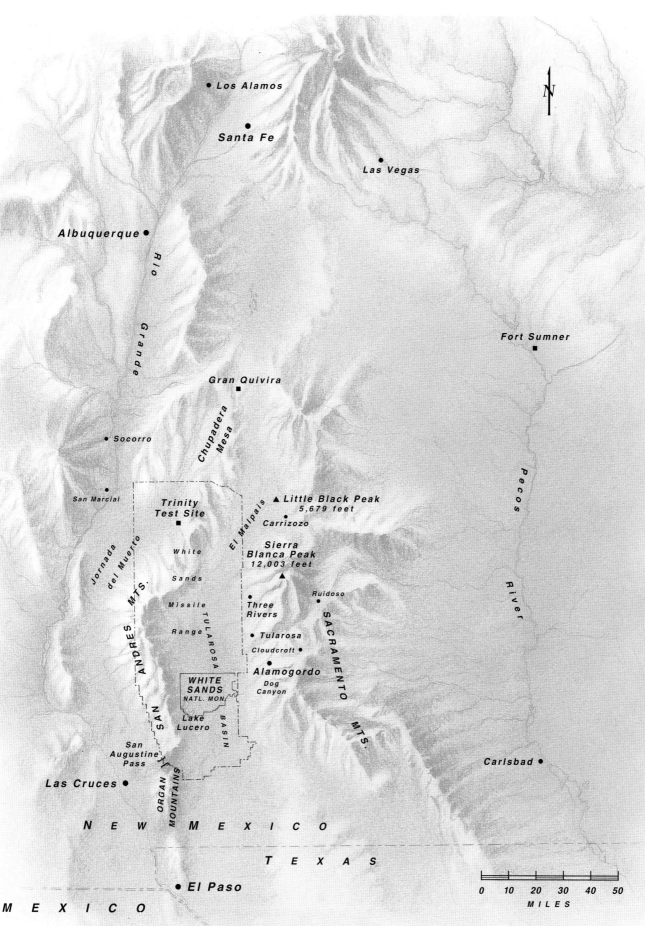

N

Los Alamos

Santa Fe

Las Vegas

Albuquerque

Rio Grande

Fort Sumner

Gran Quivira

Chupadera Mesa

Socorro

Pecos River

San Marcial

Trinity Test Site

▲ Little Black Peak
5,679 feet

El Malpais

Carrizozo

White

Jornada del Muerto

Sands

Sierra Blanca Peak
12,003 feet

▲

SAN ANDRES MTS.

Missile

Range

TULAROSA

Ruidoso

Three Rivers

SACRAMENTO MTS.

Tularosa

Cloudcroft

WHITE SANDS
NATL. MON.

Alamogordo

BASIN

Dog Canyon

Lake Lucero

San Augustine Pass

ORGAN Mountains

Carlsbad

Las Cruces

N E W   M E X I C O

T E X A S

El Paso

M E X I C O

0   10   20   30   40   50
MILES

summer of 1863 they had planted crops. Then, according to Carleton's plan, Navajos were brought in. The tension between the Apaches and Navajos, along with insects, drought, crop failures, bad food and water, and illness, plunged the Apaches into despair. Carleton steadfastly refused their requests to hunt antelope or gather mescal off the reservation.

Thus, in 1865, with famine lurking at the door of Bosque Redondo, the Apaches decided to leave as a group. On a November night they snuck from the post and scattered in all directions, confounding the army's attempts to locate

Soldiers and captive Indians, Fort Sumner, 1866.

them. (Carleton was relieved of duty the following year, and the Bosque Redondo experiment ended in failure in 1868.)

Back in Mescalero territory around the white sands, the patterns of ambushing, raiding, fighting, thievery, and retaliation by all parties resumed. Cadete had said his people would agree to settle on a reservation, if it were in their old homeland. Another ten years would pass before the Mescalero Reservation was established, on May 29, 1873, in the Sierra Blanca between Cloudcroft and Ruidoso. Two years later the boundaries were extended to include the northern Sacramentos.

The forbidding alkali desert of the Tularosa Basin was one of the last places in southern New Mexico to be settled by Anglo Americans. Unlike Anglo American settlements, most of the Native American and Hispanic towns were founded along the Rio Grande. Early Spanish travel north from El Paso either followed the Rio Grande or took the flatter, more passable route along the

Jornada del Muerto, Deadman's Journey, east of the river. The Jornada veered northeastward away from the river just beyond El Paso, headed north through the menacing arid valley on the west side of the San Andres Mountains, and rejoined the river near San Marcial, south of Socorro, New Mexico. Early Spanish maps showed the Tularosa Basin simply as "Unexplored Country."

In 1792, Hispanic travelers built a small church at La Luz, at the base of the Sacramentos, but they did not stay. During the Spanish Colonial Period between 1580 and 1821, and the twenty-seven-year Mexican Period which lasted until 1848, Hispanics engaged in some enterprising activities, such as harvesting salt from the playas. The salt was hauled in heavy wooden oxcarts, called *carretas*. In 1936, a weathered, two-hundred-year-old cart was found in the monument, exhumed by moving sands. The cart is displayed in the visitor center courtyard.

In 1862, as General Carleton was preparing to send the Mescalero Apaches to Bosque Redondo, a group of Hispanic farmers founded the town of Tularosa. Cesar Duran, Jose Candelaria, and others went there after their fields were flooded out on the Rio Grande. In Tularosa, they built adobe homes and a Catholic church, planted orchards and vineyards, and constructed *acequias* to bring water to their new fields. The town was the first permanent settlement in the Tularosa Basin. Although maps of the region began to bear more place names after that time, the white sands still were generally referred to only as the "Sand Belt with Salt Marshes & Lakes."

About fifteen years later, Texans began to move in. John Good, in the vanguard of those who migrated to the Tularosa country, set up his first ranch on Lost River. Others followed, claiming rights to grass and water. By 1889, during the days of the open range, some 85,000 head of livestock were rounded up between Three Rivers and Dog Canyon. The grazing lands were lush with grass after good moisture. As has often been the case in the Southwest, though, drought cycled through and the cattlemen suffered.

These were the days of the Wild West, when the hard-working, hard-playing cowmen observed a special code. Rancher/author Eugene Manlove Rhodes, the Bard of the Tularosa, called it the

Oliver Lee, 1940.

"rattlesnake's code, to warn before he strikes, no better; a queer, lopsided, topsy-turvy, jumbled and senseless code—but a code for all that." Fighting and killings became a nearly everyday occurrence throughout the late 1880s.

Oliver Lee, who built his Circle Cross Ranch in Dog Canyon into the largest in New Mexico, was caught in one of the fracases. He and another man were charged with the murder of local politician Albert Fountain and his son, who were killed a few miles south of the dunefield in 1896. Lee was acquitted, and the whole affair did not seem to hurt his reputation too badly. He went on to serve twice in the state legislature. (Lee's ranch house in Dog Canyon has been restored and is now part of Oliver Lee Memorial State Park.)

One of the Tularosa Basin's most famous residents and a foe of Oliver Lee was Patrick Floyd Garrett. As sheriff of Lincoln County, Pat Garrett made a name for himself by slaying Billy the Kid. Garrett, who set up a ranch at the south end of the white sands, was himself shot and killed in 1907 near San Augustin Pass.

Oliver Lee and Pat Garrett undoubtedly knew other local ranchers, the Bairds, McNews, Coxes, and Luceros. They all started their operations wherever they could dig a well and get water. W. H. McNew had a well, trough, tanks, and a windmill at Point of Sands, at the southeast edge of White Sands on the main road from Alamogordo. His was a popular watering stop for travelers.

Pat Garrett, 1898.

A road headed southwest from Point of Sands to the ranch of Jose and Felipe Lucero. These two brothers built ranches on the southwest edge of the playa lake in White Sands that now bears their name. Both were sheriffs of Dona Ana County at various times, but cattle ranching was their main occupation. Their initial 160-acre ranch was expanded to 20,000 acres. The ranch house is several miles south of Lake Lucero, but the remains of their north unit corrals, well, and windmill still stand near Lake Lucero, within the national monument, as mute evidence of the ranching era in White Sands.

In 1898, the opening of the El Paso & Northeastern Railroad brought into existence the town of Alamogordo and others along the line. Spur railroads built to serve mining and logging areas in the mountains became popular summer tourist routes as well.

The region was bustling, and ranchers fared well from 1903 to 1908, years of good water. Livestock probably grazed throughout the white sands area then; old trails and roads crossing

Jose Lucero.   Felipe Lucero.

the dunes and several water tanks and wells in remote places hint at the amount of grazing activity.

But 1909 to 1911 were dry years once again, and the penalties of possible overstocking of the range would have become apparent. By that time, too, open rangeland was a thing of the past, and public land laws and fees for grazing were tightening livestock operations.

Local folks had long been coming to the white sands to frolic in the dunes. Late nineteenth-century scientists had recognized and studied the dunes' unique geological properties. A few entrepreneurs had tried tapping the gypsum deposits to produce stucco, plaster, and cement. And in the early years of the twentieth century, another attribute was advertised—the healthful benefits of the region's dry, clear air.

One man who must have gotten wind of these salubrious health claims was Kansan Tom Charles. Seeking a cure for his wife's tuberculosis, Charles brought his family to Alamogordo in 1907. To make a go of it, Charles delivered laundry, edited the town's newspaper, homesteaded, and sold insurance. His wife died, however, and he later remarried.

Alamogordo was now Tom Charles's adopted home, and he did all he could to promote it. Charles attended meetings, wrote letters, and lobbied hard to get the white sands incorporated into plans that called for a national park of some kind in the region.

He allied himself with Albert Bacon Fall, Tularosa Basin rancher and one of New Mexico's first senators. Both as senator and later as United States Secretary of the Interior, Fall tried at least four times to secure designation of a park. The "All-Year National Park" was one that Senator Fall, Tom Charles, and other Alamogordo boosters had come closest to winning. This disjointed park idea attempted to connect various scattered sites in southern New Mexico, including 640 acres of the "gypsum hills" of the white sands. In 1923, however, Fall resigned as interior secretary because of his role in a scandal involving sale of federal oil reserves in Wyoming.

Albert Bacon Fall and Eugene Manlove Rhodes, 1930.

Tom Charles.

Tom Charles picked up where Fall left off but believed, as did many of his time, that the white sands alone could support a two-pronged economic rationale: part of it could serve as a scenic "playground" for tourists, while the rest would remain a natural resource for gypsum miners. By 1929, Charles was pushing the idea of a white sands national monument, rather than a national park, that would include only a portion of the sand dunes. In 1931, the National Park Service completed a study of the area's worthiness, and in January 1933, outgoing President Herbert

Hoover proclaimed 142,987 acres of white sands as a national monument.

Tom Charles was present on April 29, 1934, when at least four thousand people attended the official dedication and opening of the national monument. Considered "Mr. White Sands" by many, Charles was hired as the monument's first custodian, at a starting salary of four dollars a month. One of his jobs was to count the rapidly expanding number of visitors, which rose from twelve thousand in 1933 to nearly one hundred thousand in 1936.

With the Great Depression stifling the country, President Franklin Roosevelt sent men and women employed by his New Deal programs to White Sands to build facilities. Among those projects was the new park road. Another was the visitor center and museum. Completed in 1938, this graceful adobe structure with large pine beams is of the Pueblo-Revival style of architecture. The visitor center and several other buildings nearby are on the National Register of Historic Places.

In 1939, Tom Charles left his custodian job and began the White Sands Service Company. As a concessionaire, he took people on bus and auto tours into the dunes until 1943, when he became ill and died. He did not live to witness one of the most significant events of history that would soon occur near his beloved sand dunes at a place called Trinity.

White Sands National Monument visitor center, 1944.

Dedication of White Sands National Monument, April 29, 1934.

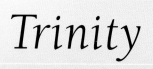

Trinity

At 5:29 on the morning of July 16, 1945, a light flashed across the New Mexico desert so bright that it was seen from Arizona to Texas. A blind college girl, riding in a car near Socorro in those dawn hours, asked what the flash of light was. Unknown to her and to most of the rest of the world at that moment, the light resulted from the explosion of a plutonium bomb, a test known as "Trinity," in the Jornada del Muerto sixty-five miles northwest of White Sands.

The people present at the test still remember the brilliant light most vividly. That light represented the imminent end of World War II, and it changed the world forever.

The United States government had decided that this lonely part of New Mexico was ideal terrain for military operations. The Trinity Test Site was located within the Alamogordo Bombing and Gunnery Range, established in 1942, just after the attack on Pearl Harbor. Following the

Bomb atop 100-foot tower at ground zero.

test in 1945 additional portions of the Tularosa Basin were set aside as White Sands Proving Ground. The gunnery range and proving ground were consolidated and renamed White Sands Missile Range in 1958.

It all began in June 1942, when the United States government launched the top-secret

Manhattan Project in a race to beat the Germans, who were believed to be building their own bomb. The bomb detonated at the Trinity site had been designed at the newly created Los Alamos Laboratory north of Santa Fe. Dr. J. Robert Oppenheimer was the physicist who headed the Manhattan Project; General Leslie Groves was the military overseer. One story says that the erudite Oppenheimer selected the code name "Trinity," from a sonnet by John Donne:

Batter my heart, three-person'd God; for, you As yet but knock, breathe, shine, and seek to mend...

The poetry may have offered comfort from the truth of the ultimate use of an atomic bomb as the most devastating weapon of war then known to humankind.

There were actually two designs for an atomic bomb, one for a plutonium bomb and a simpler one for a uranium bomb which would not need testing. The theory behind the plutonium design, selected for the Trinity test, was to surround the plutonium with conventional TNT, all encased in thick steel. The TNT would be set off first, exploding inward and triggering a nuclear chain reaction created by the splitting of billions of atoms within a millionth of a second. No one was certain that it would work,

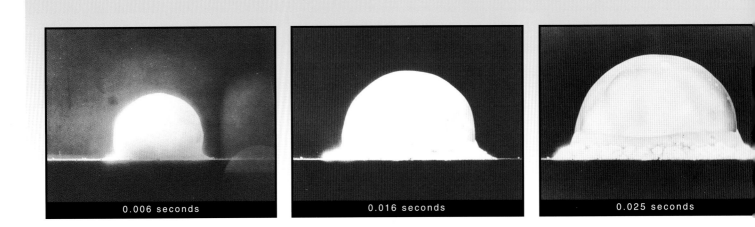

0.006 seconds   0.016 seconds   0.025 seconds

Tower at ground zero.

until that morning at Trinity.

A makeshift base camp was set up at the Trinity site by early 1945, and scientists and personnel readied for the test. By May they had staged their first rehearsal. General Groves had a journalist prepare four press releases to cover the possible outcomes of the test, describing scenarios ranging from no property damage or loss of life to the worst case of widespread destruction of property and great loss of life.

Finally, on Friday, July 13, the core and the trigger, or initiator, the most critical and still uncertain piece of the bomb, were assembled in a nearby ranch house. Then the core was driven, very carefully, in a sedan to a one-hundred-foot-high steel tower, where the entire bomb was put together. On July 14 the "thing" or the "gadget," as the bomb was called, was hoisted to a wooden platform at the top of the tower. At the last minute, mattresses were piled beneath it, at ground zero, should the thing accidentally fall.

Breakfast at base camp was at 3:45 a.m. on July 16. The test was scheduled for 4 a.m., but had to be delayed because it was raining. As the weather broke, the long-awaited countdown started at 5:10 a.m. Oppenheimer, anxious and haggard, waited with a few others in shelters ten thousand yards away from ground zero. They were issued welders' goggles and told to lie on their stomachs, facing away from ground zero. Most, however, would watch from Compania Hill twenty miles to the northwest.

At zero minus five minutes, the men hit the trenches. A siren wailed, and a warning rocket was shot into the air. At zero minus one, another rocket flare. At exactly 5:29:45, Mountain War Time, the bomb was detonated. Within milliseconds, an orangish-red fireball swept over the desert and hurled into the sky. A mushroom

Oppenheimer and Groves at ground zero, September 1945.

cloud of gray and purple towered thirty-eight thousand feet into the atmosphere. Thundering shock waves from the nineteen-kiloton blast broke windows 120 miles away.

0.053 seconds   2 seconds   10 seconds

The initial story given to the populace was that munitions had been set off on the gunnery range. But the truth would soon be known. On August 6, a uranium bomb was dropped on Hiroshima, Japan. On that day, President Harry Truman announced to the world what had happened at Trinity. Three days later, another bomb, like the one tested at Trinity, was dropped on Nagasaki. Nearly one hundred thousand Japanese were injured or killed. On August 14 Japan surrendered and the war was over.

In the next ten years, the defense establishment boomed in a way that had never been seen in the remote Tularosa Basin. Thousands of people moved onto military bases. "The lonesome cowboys of 1885, or even 1935," wrote historian Leland Sonnichsen, "could not recognize their home ranges." Many did not give up their ranches or their way of life easily to the military.

White Sands National Monument was initially threatened by the imposing military development on its boundaries. But through a series of permits, it has developed a strong working relationship with defense department neighbors. Today, a memorandum of agreement governs the military's use of the western half of the monument. Several branches of the armed services and other federal agencies, such as the National Aeronautics and Space Administration, now operate and test on the White Sands Missile Range. In 1982, the space shuttle *Columbia* landed at the White Sands Space Harbor.

To protect visitors from wayward missiles, the monument is closed on certain days, sometimes on short notice. Visitors walking in the dunes are advised not to handle missile parts that occasionally land in the sands.

Atomic bomb explosion at Trinity, July 16, 1945.

VISITING TRINITY

At the entrance to the Trinity Test Site sits Jumbo, the 214-ton steel vessel designed to contain the plutonium core of the bomb. Although Jumbo was not used as intended, i did survive the blast eight hundred yards away. Within a chain link fence, a simple obelisk of basalt rock marks ground zero. Nothing remains of the steel tower where the bomb was suspended; it vaporized fractions of a second after the blast. The depression made by the blast has been backfilled.

People listen attentively to guides who relate the story of the Manhattan Project and the Trinity test. They file quietly past black-and-white photographs mounted on the fence which show the swift sequence of the actual blast. A few carry Geiger counters to measure the radiation levels, about ten times background levels. They peer through the glass of a bunker which contains leftover

Jumbo, July 1945.

chunks of trinitite, the jade-colored glass that resulted when the desert sands were fused by the heat of the blast. Most of the trinitite was removed from the site to reduce radiation.

Buses carry visitors the mile from ground zero to the George McDonald Ranch House, restored with the help of the National Park Service. In the northeast room of this single-story adobe house the atomic bomb was assembled. In the blast, the windows of the ranch house were blown out, and the roof of the barn fell in.

Designated a National Historic Landmark in 1975, the Trinity site is open twice a year to the public, on the first Saturday of April and the first Saturday in October. Contact White Sands Public Affairs Office (505-678-1134), or the Alamogordo Chamber of Commerce (1-800-545-4021 out of state, or 1-800-826-0294 within New Mexico) for information on tours.

Visiting White Sands National Monument

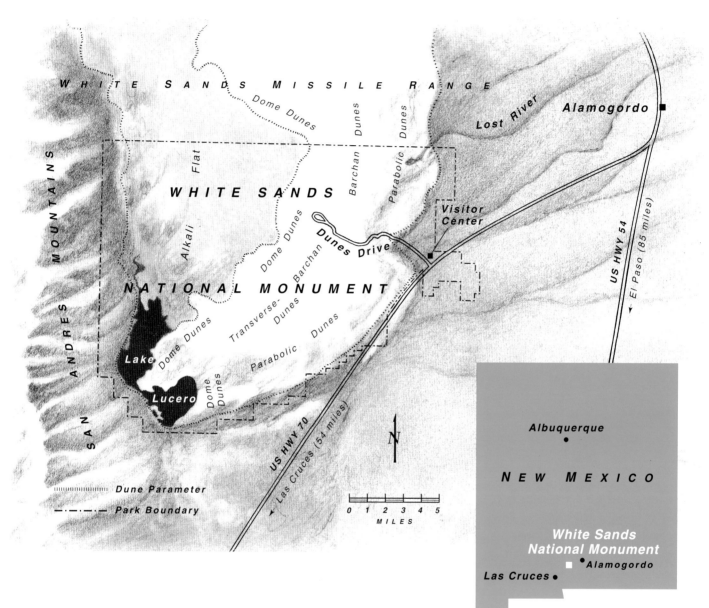

YOUR FIRST STOP SHOULD BE the White Sands National Monument Visitor Center, which includes a museum, information desk, bookstore, gift shop, and restrooms.

An eight-mile scenic drive leads from the visitor center into the heart of the dunes. Wayside exhibits at pullouts along the drive provide information about the natural history of the park. Numerous parking areas along the drive allow visitors to stop and explore the dunes on foot.

Picnic areas with sheltered tables are located at the end of the scenic drive and are available on a first-come-first-served basis. No alcohol is permitted in the park from February 1 through May 31. No water is available anywhere along the dunes drive. There are no campgrounds in the frontcountry of the park. Both public and private campgrounds are available in the area. A backcountry campsite is available in the park. Please register at the visitor center upon arrival to use this site.

White Sands National Monument is open daily, except Christmas Day, from 8 a.m. until sunset. During the summer, the park remains open until 9 p.m.

Readings

Atkinson, Richard. *White Sands: Wind, Sand and Time*. Tucson, Arizona: Southwest
    Parks and Monuments Association. 1977.

Bowers, Janice Emily. *Seasons of the Wind*. Flagstaff, Arizona: Northland Press. 1986.

Findley, James S. *The Natural History of New Mexican Mammals*. Albuquerque.
    University of New Mexico Press. 1987.

Lamont, Lansing. *Day of Trinity*. New York: Atheneum. 1985.

McKee, Edwin D. "Growth and Movement of Dunes at White Sands National
    Monument, New Mexico." *U.S. Geological Survey Professional Paper 750-D*,
    pp 108-114. 1971.

Meinzer, O.E. and R.F. Hare. "Geology and Water Resources of Tularosa Basin, New
    Mexico." *U.S. Geological Survey Water-Supply Paper 343*. Washington, D.C.:
    1915.

Reid, William, coord. "White Sands National Monument: Natural Resources
    Inventory and Analyses, Final Report." *Laboratory for Environmental Biology,
    Research Report 11*, Biological Sciences, University of Texas El Paso. August
    1979.

Schneider-Hector, Dietmar. *White Sands: The History of a National Monument*.
    Albuquerque: University of New Mexico Press. 1993.

Sonnichsen, C. L. *The Mescalero Apaches*. Norman: University of Oklahoma Press.
    1973.

_____. *Tularosa: Last of the Frontier West*. Albuquerque: University of New
    Mexico Press. 1980.

Technical Manual. "1973 Survey of the Tularosa Basin." Human Systems Research, Inc.

Zwinger, Ann Haymond. *The Mysterious Lands*. New York: Truman Talley
    Books/Plume. 1989.